COOKING YOUR WAY THROUGH AMERICAN HISTORY

RECIPES OF THE WESTWARD EXPANSION

By Nick Christopher

KidHaven
PUBLISHING

Published in 2017 by
KidHaven Publishing, an Imprint of Greenhaven Publishing, LLC
353 3rd Avenue
Suite 255
New York, NY 10010

Designer: Seth Hughes
Editor: Jennifer Lombardo

Photo credits:
Cover (bottom) Currier and Ives/Getty Images; cover (top), p. 9 (skillet bread) Brent Hofacker/Shutterstock.com; back cover, pp. 2, 3, 9, 13, 19, 22-24 (wood texture) Maya Kruchankova/Shutterstock.com; p. 4 courtesy of Wikimedia Commons; p. 5 Hannah Eckman/Shutterstock.com; p. 7 sergioboccardo/Shutterstock.com; pp. 9, 13, 19 (notebook) BrAt82/Shutterstock.com; p. 11 Charles Phelps Cushing/ClassicStock/Getty Images; p. 13 (sardines) Digivic/Shutterstock.com; p. 13 (beans) William Berry/Shutterstock.com; p. 13 (crackers) SOMMAI/Shutterstock.com; p. 15 Neil Lockhart/Shutterstock.com; p. 17 SuperStock/Shutterstock.com; p. 19 (beans and rice) © istockphoto.com/villorejo; p. 21 Autumn's Memories/Shutterstock.com

Cataloging-in-Publication Data

Names: Christopher, Nick.
Title: Recipes of the westward expansion / Nick Christopher.
Description: New York : KidHaven Publishing, 2017. | Series: Cooking your way through American history| Includes index.
Identifiers: ISBN 9781534521001 (pbk.) | ISBN 9781534521025 (library bound) | ISBN 9781534521018 (6 pack) | ISBN 9781534521032 (ebook)
Subjects: LCSH: Cooking, American–History–Juvenile literature. | West (U.S.)–Discovery and exploration–Juvenile literature. | United States–Territorial expansion–Juvenile literature.
Classification: LCC TX715.C45 2017 | DDC 641.5'0973'09034–dc23

CPSIA compliance information: Batch #CW17KL: For further information contact Greenhaven Publishing LLC, New York, New York at 1-844-317-7404.

Please visit our website, www.greenhavenpublishing.com. For a free color catalog of all our high-quality books, call toll free 1-844-317-7404 or fax 1-844-317-7405.

CONTENTS

THE OREGON TRAIL

In 1803, President Thomas Jefferson bought land in North America that France owned. This made the United States twice as big as it had been. People started to move out of the crowded cities and go west, where they could start their own farms. Adam was nine years old in 1845, when he and his family headed for the Oregon Territory, on the West Coast of North America. They were looking for cheap, **fertile** land where they could raise cattle.

The pioneers rode west in wagons that were pulled by oxen and covered with **canvas** to keep rain off of the supplies in the wagon. All the pioneers who were going west at one time traveled together in a wagon train so they would be protected from the dangers of the trail, such as wild animals or bandits.

Thomas Jefferson

The pioneers traveled west in covered wagons.

LIFE ON THE TRAIL

The wagon that belonged to Adam's family was full of the supplies they needed to last the whole trip. It was so full that Adam and his family had to walk next to the wagon. Only people who were too sick or too young to walk could ride inside the wagons. Some families they met along the way could only afford to bring flour, **cornmeal**, bacon, beans, coffee, sugar, and salt. Adam's family brought those supplies, as well as rice, dried fruits and vegetables, **molasses**, and beef fat. If people ran out of food on the trip, there were **forts** along the way where they could trade for more.

Adam's family didn't have fresh meat until they reached the first bison herds in the Midwest. Then Adam's father hunted and killed a bison. Adam's mother cooked some of the meat and dried the rest of it to save for the trip. The pioneers also hunted deer, antelope, and birds. When they were near water, they could sometimes catch fish.

Bison was an important part of meals for Native Americans and pioneers.

PIONEER COOKING

At night, the wagons would stop and make a circle for protection. The pioneers would light fires inside the circle so they could cook dinner. The only cooking tools Adam's mother brought were a heavy iron **kettle**, skillet, small pot, wooden spoon, and eating **utensils**. The rest of the wagon was filled with food, clothing, and farming tools.

Some pioneers brought a Dutch oven with them, which was a small iron cooking pot with a tight-fitting cover. Food would be placed in the Dutch oven, which would then be put into the fire. People who didn't have room in their wagons for a Dutch oven would cook in a skillet or kettle over the fire, or bake things in the coals. Sometimes the women would make stew. In the morning, they would wake up early to make beans, pancakes, and coffee for breakfast so the wagons could start moving by the time the sun rose.

skillet bread

Ingredients:

1 ¼ cups milk
1 tablespoon lemon juice
¾ cup all-purpose flour
1 teaspoon salt
1 teaspoon baking powder
1 teaspoon baking soda
2 tablespoons cold vegetable shortening

Directions:

- Preheat the oven to 400° Fahrenheit (F).
- Make buttermilk by pouring the milk and lemon juice into a small bowl. Stir, and let it sit for five minutes.
- Sift the flour, salt, baking powder, and baking soda into a medium-size bowl.
- Mix the vegetable shortening with the flour mixture by cutting it into tiny pieces with two knives.
- Add half of the buttermilk, and mix the dough with your fingers. Keep adding buttermilk and mixing just until the dough sticks together. Let the dough sit for five minutes.
- Lightly grease the bottom and sides of an 8x8-inch baking pan with shortening. Dip your fingers in flour, and spread the dough evenly in the pan.
- Bake for 35 minutes, or until the top is brown. Serve warm with butter or jam.

This serves four people.

The pioneers would use a skillet to make this bread, but today it's easier to bake it in the oven. Remember to always ask an adult for help when cooking.

THE GOLD RUSH

The pioneers settled when they found a place they liked. Adam's family settled in what's now the state of Idaho. Adam's father learned that the land was good for growing wheat and raising cattle. Adam's family used the cattle they raised for meat, milk, cheese, and butter. They ate these themselves and also sold them to other people, including people passing through on their way to California.

Gold was discovered in California in 1848. Thousands of **prospectors** traveled to California in search of gold. Adam's Uncle Ben was one of them. Adam learned from his Uncle Ben that prospectors lived in a very different way than the settlers. Uncle Ben lived in a mining camp with other prospectors in what's now northern California. He had few belongings, but he did own a skillet and a kettle for heating water. He ate simple food that he called "grub."

Mining companies hired workers to look for gold.

WHAT DID PROSPECTORS EAT?

Some prospectors found a lot of gold and became rich. Those people could afford to eat in the restaurants people were opening in California. However, Uncle Ben, like most prospectors, wasn't rich. Women did all the cooking at that time, and since prospectors were all men, many of them didn't know how to cook for themselves. Before he started living in the mining camp, Uncle Ben's meals were often made up of bread, canned beans, bacon, and strong coffee. As a treat, he ate canned sardines. Uncle Ben hardly ever ate fruit, vegetables, milk, cheese, or eggs because they were expensive.

Because Uncle Ben didn't like to cook or wash dishes, he generally cooked canned food right in the can on his stove or over a fire. He even ate the food out of the can! He would sometimes make dough out of flour and water, then pull off small, round pieces and fry them in hot bacon grease.

Uncle Ben's dinner

Ingredients:

4 slices bacon
1 16-ounce can of pork and beans
1 can of sardines, packed in oil
crackers

Directions:

- Fry the bacon in a medium-size frying pan until it's crispy.
- Take the bacon out of the pan, and put it on a plate covered with a paper towel.
- Pour most of the bacon fat into an old can or jar. Leave a little on the bottom of the pan to flavor the beans.
- Put the pan back on the heat, and empty the can of beans into the pan. Stir until they begin to bubble.
- When the beans are hot, pour some onto your plate.
- Put a few sardines and the bacon next to the beans.
- Serve with crackers. This serves one person.

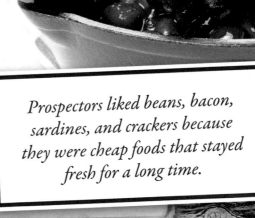

Prospectors liked beans, bacon, sardines, and crackers because they were cheap foods that stayed fresh for a long time.

FOOD IN THE MINING CAMPS

Mining companies would build camps in areas where prospectors found a **seam** of gold. The company would then hire people to remove the gold from the mines. Uncle Ben was never lucky enough to find much gold on his own, so he worked in the mines. He wrote to Adam to tell him what it was like living in the camp.

Many of the miners were Chinese men who had left their country to try to find a better life in the United States. The miners worked hard, and they ate a lot. The camp had a real kitchen and several dining houses. The cooks made soups, stews, roasted meats, and boiled potatoes with other vegetables. They also baked fresh breads, pies, and cakes. They made eggs, ham, bacon, toast, and hot porridge with canned milk for breakfast. The dining house charged money for the food, but since the miners were getting paid, they could generally afford it.

Mining companies built cabins for their workers to live in. When the gold rush ended, everyone moved away, and the empty camps were called ghost towns.

LIFE AS A COWBOY

Because they had a cattle ranch, Adam's family hired cowboys to help out. The cowboys would ride on horses and make sure the cattle kept moving in the right direction. This was called driving the cattle. Sometimes the cowboys would drive the herd thousands of miles, from the ranch to the market.

The cowboys called their food "chuck." They carried it with them in sacks that hung from their saddles if they only planned to camp out for two or three days. They generally brought bread, bacon, salt, and coffee with them. However, if they were going longer distances and needed food for months at a time, they would travel with a chuck wagon. A cook drove the wagon, which carried a large chest of food, water, pots, pans, and wood or **cow chips** to light the fire with. The cook traveled ahead of the cowboys and the cattle. Each night, he parked at that night's camping spot. He had dinner ready when the cowboys arrived.

Cowboys worked hard all day, so they were happy to have dinner ready for them in the evening.

WHAT DID COWBOYS EAT?

There were no refrigerators in the chuck wagon, so the cowboys brought meat such as salt pork and bacon, which would stay good longer than fresh meat. They also brought beef jerky to snack on. Often, they would kill one of the cows and have steak or beef stew. Sometimes the cowboys would hunt wild animals or go fishing in the rivers, but they didn't have time to do this often.

Many of the foods the cowboys ate were canned or dried. The cook served beans almost every day because beans kept fresh for a long time. Red beans were popular; the cowboys called them "**prairie** strawberries." The cook would also serve rice or potatoes, cornmeal mush, chili, and biscuits or bread. Sometimes he would make apple pie as a special treat. The cowboys loved coffee, so it was served with every meal.

red beans 'n rice

Ingredients:

2 ½ cups dried red beans
1 medium onion, diced
2 tablespoons vegetable oil
½ teaspoon salt
½ teaspoon onion salt
½ teaspoon garlic powder
½ teaspoon pepper
4 cups water
2 cups cooked rice

Directions:

- Soak the beans in a pot of water overnight. Drain them when you're ready to cook.
- Sauté the onion in oil in a medium-size pot until the pieces are almost clear.
- Add the beans, salt, onion salt, garlic powder, pepper, and water.
- Bring the beans to a boil over medium heat.
- Stir, and lower the heat. Simmer for two hours.
- Serve the beans over cooked rice.

This serves about four people.

Beans and rice were two foods that the cowboys ate at almost every meal. The chuck wagon carried a lot of them because they stayed fresh for a long time.

CHANGES IN THE UNITED STATES

When people started moving west, many things changed in the United States. New states were added, and settlers similar to Adam's family were able to move out of the crowded cities and own land in the new territory. There were plenty of animals to hunt and fish to catch. It seemed like there was enough food and land for everyone.

However, the land the settlers were moving onto belonged to Native Americans. These groups were forced by the United States government to live on small areas of land called **reservations**. Today, many Native Americans still live on reservations.

The Westward Expansion and the gold rush combined many different kinds of people on the West Coast. The pioneers and prospectors from the East Coast and the Chinese **immigrants** brought their foods and cultures with them, which is why the West Coast is such a **diverse** place today.

Many Native Americans still live on reservations that belong to their people.

ENTERING
NAVAJO RESERVATION
U. S. DEPT. INTERIOR

RIVER

COLORADO

UTAH   COLORADO
ARIZONA   NEW MEXICO

FLAGSTAFF

GLOSSARY

canvas: A strong, rough cloth that is used to make bags, tents, and sails.

cornmeal: A coarse flour made from crushed corn.

cow chips: Dried cow dung.

diverse: Made up of people or things that are different from each other.

fertile: Good for growing plants.

fort: A strong building or group of buildings where soldiers live.

immigrants: People who come to a country to live there.

kettle: A container used for heating or boiling.

molasses: A thick, brown, sweet liquid that is made from raw sugar.

prairie: A large, mostly flat area of land in North America that has few trees and is covered in grasses.

prospectors: People who explore an area in search of gold.

reservations: Land set aside by the government for specific Native American groups to live on.

seam: A bed of valuable mineral.

utensil: A simple and useful device that is used for doing tasks in a person's home and especially in the kitchen.

FOR MORE INFORMATION

WEBSITES

Food of the California Gold Rush
www.pbs.org/food/the-history-kitchen/food-california-gold-rush/
Learn more about what prospectors and miners ate during the gold rush.

The Other Pioneers: African-Americans on the Frontier
www.scholastic.com/browse/article.jsp?id=4807
Pioneers, miners, and cowboys are often shown as white men in movies and on TV, but many of them were black, Mexican, and Asian. On this website, learn more about why life on the frontier was especially hard for black men and women.

Westward Expansion and the Old West
www.ducksters.com/history/westward_expansion/
Articles include information about the gold rush, the first transcontinental railroad, the Louisiana Purchase, daily life on the frontier, and more!

BOOKS

Machajewski, Sarah. *A Kid's Life During the Westward Expansion.* New York, NY: PowerKids Press, 2015.

Sheinkin, Steve. *Which Way to the Wild West?: Everything Your Schoolbooks Didn't Tell You About Westward Expansion.* New York, NY: Square Fish, 2015.

Wilson, Steve. *The California Gold Rush: Chinese Laborers in America (1848-1882).* New York, NY: PowerKids Press, 2016.

INDEX

B
bacon, 6, 12, 13, 14, 16, 18
beans, 6, 8, 12, 13, 18, 19
bison, 6, 7

C
California, 10, 12
canned food, 12, 14, 18
cattle, 4, 10, 16
coffee, 6, 8, 12, 16, 18
cornmeal, 6, 18
cowboys, 16, 17, 18, 19

D
Dutch oven, 8

F
fish, 6, 18, 20
fruit, 6, 12

G
gold, 10, 11, 12, 14
gold rush, 10, 15, 20
grub, 10

H
hunt, 6, 18, 20

J
Jefferson, Thomas, 4

K
kettle, 8, 10

M
mining camp, 10, 12, 14

N
Native Americans, 7, 20, 21

O
Oregon Territory, 4

P
prospector, 10, 12, 13, 14, 20

R
reservations, 20, 21

S
skillet, 8, 9, 10

V
vegetables, 6, 12, 14

W
wagon, 4, 5, 6, 8, 16, 18, 19